ICT

Writing Programs

Anne Rooney

QED Publishing

First published in the UK in 2004 by
QED Publishing
A Quarto Group Company
226 City Road
London, EC1V 2TT

www.qed-publishing.co.uk

A Catalogue record for this book is available
from the British Library.

ISBN 1 84538 271 4

Written by Anne Rooney
Consultant Philip Stubbs
Designed by Jacqueline Palmer
Editor Anna Claybourne
Illustrator John Haslam
Photographer Ray Moller
Models supplied by Scallywags

Creative Director Louise Morley
Editorial Manager Jean Coppendale

Printed and bound in China

The words in **bold** are
explained in the Glossary
on page 31.

Contents

What's it all about?

All around you, computers and other machines are hard at work, doing all kinds of different jobs. But how do they know what to do? It's all down to the instructions we put into them.

Machines at home

Your house is probably full of equipment that follows instructions – like your remote control TV, microwave oven and programmable washing machine.

But there's plenty more. Some types of equipment watch for changes or events, and then carry out an action. The heating starts up when the temperature drops, and the light in the fridge comes on when you open the fridge door. These are examples of **control technology**, and they work using a **control sequence**.

Responding to events

You can spot a control sequence by looking out for anything that responds to some kind of event by carrying out instructions that make something happen.

The event could be information you give or an action you take, such as pressing the buttons on the microwave oven or turning a switch.

Or it could be information the equipment gains from the environment around it, like the temperature, the amount of light or whether anything is moving.

Time to take control!

In this book, you'll find out how control sequences work, and how to use a set of instructions to make something happen. You'll also look at ways of making things happen if something else happens – like making a light come on when it gets dark.

How does it work?

When you go to the supermarket, you tread on a special mat on the floor and the door opens for you. This is an example of a control sequence. Let's take a closer look at how it works...

Input and output

In the supermarket door control sequence, the event that makes the door open is your weight on the mat. This is called the **input** to the system.

The instructions tell the door 'if someone stands on the mat, open the door'.

The door opening is the result — it's called the **output**.

Input

Output

Input

Output

More inputs and outputs

Types of input include things such as changes in temperature, the amount of humidity (water in the air) and certain types of movement – or more obvious events like someone pressing a button.

Types of output are things such as moving an object, making a sound or turning a light on or off. In some cars, the windscreen wipers turn on if the windscreen senses rain. Rain is the input; moving the wipers is the output.

Get it right

Let's go back to the supermarket. The instruction 'if someone stands on the mat, open the door' is not quite as simple as it looks. The door must open if something heavy enough to be a person treads on the mat. But the door shouldn't open if a bee lands on it, or a bit of rubbish blows onto it.

And how heavy is a person? Should the door open if a light person – a child – treads on the mat? Maybe not at the exit, or small children might be able to run away.

What do you want to do?

A set of instructions to control something can be called a control sequence or a **program**. Writing instructions is called **programming**.

Turtle technology

If you work on control technology at school, you'll probably start by working with a floor turtle or tortoise. It's a simple robot that moves around on the floor according to the instructions – or programs – that you give it.

You might also use computer software that works in the same way, following your instructions to draw lines or patterns on the screen.

Think first

Before you start giving instructions, think about what you want to achieve! That might sound obvious, but remember that any computer or electrical device can only do exactly what you tell it. It can't make any decisions for itself.

So you can't just say 'turn the heating on if it gets cold' – you have to decide exactly what temperature counts as 'cold'.

Once you've worked out what you want to happen (the output) and what is going to make it happen (the input), you can write the instructions you need.

Using sensors

Many control systems, like the supermarket door, act on information from their surroundings. They have **sensors** – devices that can detect things like light, pressure or temperature.

If you want a light to come on when it gets dark, for example, you'll need an electrical circuit with a light sensor that can sense light levels. This type of system **monitors** the environment – it keeps checking whether it's dark and turns the light on if it is.

Hmm! It's getting darker...

Dark enough – time to switch on!

Writing instructions

Now let's have a look at how you can give instructions to a floor turtle to make it follow a particular route.

Lettuce quest

Imagine you wanted to move the turtle from where it is to the lettuce.

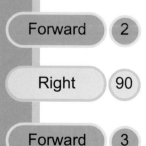

The turtle can only go up, down, left or right. To get there quickly, it could go:

- Up three squares, then left two

or

- Left two squares, then up three

Tell the turtle

To make a floor turtle or tortoise do something like this, you need to use the buttons on it to give it the right instructions. To take the second route, for example, you'd need to press these buttons:

Forward 2 — 'Forward 2' tells the turtle to go forward two spaces.

Right 90 — 'Right 90' tells it to turn 90 degrees to the right.

Forward 3 — 'Forward 3' tells it to go forward another three spaces.

Go — The 'Go' button tells the turtle the instructions are finished, and it can start to carry them out.

On the screen

Instead of a floor turtle, you might use a computer program such as **Logo** to draw a route on the screen. This will have extra instructions, such as 'Pendown' (start drawing lines) and 'Penup' (stop drawing).

These instructions draw a square:

Pendown

Forward 4

Right 90

Forward 4

Right 90

Forward 4

Right 90

Forward 4

Penup

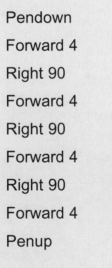

Leave a space

If you move the screen turtle or pen after a 'penup' instruction, a line is not drawn. You can use this to leave a space before doing the next bit of your drawing. For example, this program draws a line, leaves a space, and draws another line.

Pendown

Forward 2

Penup

Forward 1

Pendown

Forward 2

Penup

Do it again!

You'll often want to use the same instructions again and again. You don't need to type in the same instructions lots of times, though – you can tell the screen turtle to repeat an instruction.

Make a loop

To draw a square, you can use the same instruction several times. This is called a **loop** or a **repeat**. So instead of the sequence shown on page 11, you could write:

```
Pendown
Repeat 3
[Forward 4
Right 90]
Forward 4
Penup
```

This tells the computer to repeat the instructions 'Forward 4, Right 90' three times, then draw a final line to complete the square.

Give it a name

If you want to use the same set of instructions again and again, you can give it a name. When you've done this, you can use it just by typing its name.

A set of instructions with a name is called a **procedure**. If we called the procedure to draw a square 'square', we could then draw lots of squares with spaces in between them, like this:

```
Square
Forward 2
Square
Forward 2
Square
```

Remember that the 'penup' instruction at the end of the square procedure means no line is drawn until the next 'pendown'.

DO IT!

There are different versions of Logo and other similar programs, so you'll have to find out the exact instructions yours uses. Find out which type of brackets you need to use – it might be (and) or [and].

If you can repeat shapes, and you can leave spaces between them or turn the pen or turtle around between them, you can easily draw patterns.

Drawing shapes

So far, you've drawn squares and lines. Here are some more shapes to try:

Triangle

You can draw a triangle by changing the angles the turtle turns at:

```
Pendown
Repeat 3
[Forward 8
Right 120]
Penup
```

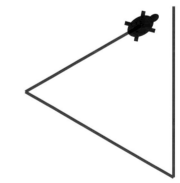

Rectangle

You can draw a rectangle by drawing two long sides and two short sides:

```
Pendown
Repeat 2
[Forward 4
Right 90
Forward 2
Right 90]
Penup
```

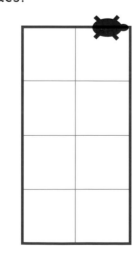

Remember that your turtle is turning around the outside of each corner of the triangle.

Mystery shape

Can you work out from reading the program what this shape will look like?

```
Pendown
Repeat 360
[Forward 1
Right 1]
Penup
```

Make a windmill

You can draw a windmill by repeating a triangle four times, turning 90 degrees each time.

You'd start by writing a procedure to draw a triangle, then use it with a 90 degree turn, repeating four times:

```
Pendown
Repeat 4
[Triangle
Right 90]
Penup
```

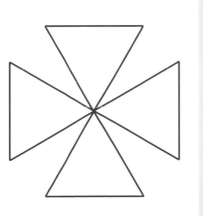

It's snowing!

If you use 'penup' to stop drawing while you move the pen or screen turtle, you can draw a shape like this:

You could save this as a procedure called 'snowflake' and then draw it six times to make a snowflake:

Testing, testing

Drawing more complicated shapes can be tricky, and you might make a few mistakes to start with. Don't worry – this happens even to people who write computer programs for a living! Always test your programs to avoid problems.

Step by step

All sets of instructions need to be tested to make sure they work. And if you're using loops or procedures, it's best to try out each step to make sure it works before you go any further.

Separate parts

Suppose you wanted to draw a row of houses, like this:

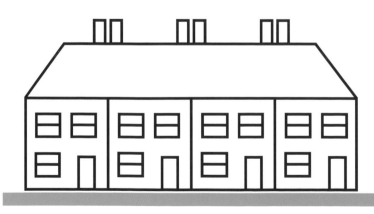

You would write procedures to draw the chimneys, windows and doors as different types of box. Try out all the procedures separately, before writing the whole set of instructions, to make sure they work.

Looking for mistakes

If your instructions don't work, either nothing will happen, or the wrong thing will happen. You'll need to find out why. There might be a message telling you where the instructions have gone wrong, which will help you find the mistake.

Look for:

• Spelling mistakes

If you've used the wrong word, missed out a space or spelled a word wrongly, your instructions won't work.

What's a squarw?

• Wrong numbers

If you move the pen the wrong number of spaces or turn through the wrong angle, it won't draw the shape you want.

• Missing something out

If you miss something out — like a turn, a number, a bracket or a procedure — you won't get what you expect.

Ask a friend to check your program to see if they can spot any problems.

Planning a sequence

In everyday life, you're surrounded by devices that are part of control sequences. They all follow lists of instructions and procedures.

Plan it

When programmers write instructions to make a sequence work, they have to plan carefully. Before programming a set of traffic lights, they'd ask:

- In what order do the lights come on?

- How long does each light stay on for?

- Are any two lights on at the same time?

- What makes the lights change?

- Will the lights work 24 hours a day?

It's often easiest to plan a control sequence by drawing a storyboard – a set of drawings that show all the different stages.

DO IT!

Try drawing your own storyboard showing a sequence of traffic lights coming on in different combinations. Think about how you could write a program to make this happen.

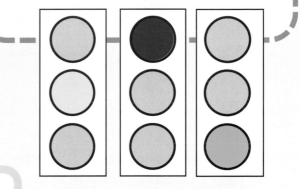

Perfect timing

Many control sequences work on time intervals. The traffic lights have to be set to stay red or green a sensible length of time, and the timing in the instructions needs to be carefully matched to the traffic patterns.

If you've got a simple control box and some **electrical components**, you could even try making a set of working lights.

Often, the timing on traffic lights changes during the day, so that traffic going into town gets more time in the morning, and traffic coming out gets more time in the evening when everyone is going home. Getting it wrong will cause people to become cross and impatient, and could even lead to accidents.

Triggering events

Control technologies work by using an input to **trigger** an event, or make something happen. The input can come from a person, or it can be detected automatically.

Switches and sensors

A system operated by a switch works when someone presses the switch — so, for example, a pedestrian light changes when a person presses the button. If no one wants to cross the road, the lights don't change.

Other systems use sensors to decide when to work. A sensor detects changes — such as differences in light, noise or pressure.

So:

An alarm in an art gallery might go off if a light beam is broken by someone leaning too close to a picture.

A sprinkler comes on if it senses smoke.

An automatic cat flap opens when it senses signals from a transmitter on the cat's collar.

Monitoring changes

Some sensors monitor changes in the environment. You could use a thermometer as a sensor to see how the temperature changes over the day or year.

Sometimes, sensors are connected to computers so that the computer can take readings automatically at regular intervals.

Temperature in Classroom 4X

25°C
20°C
15°C
10°C
5°C
0°C
midnight 4am 8am noon 4pm 8pm midnight
Time of day

Connecting a sensor to a computer means you can make readings without having to be there all the time. For example, you could measure the temperature at school all night long.

 ## DO IT!

Find out how to link a sensor to a computer. Make sure you know how to set the interval for monitoring and how to read the recordings. Then monitor the temperature, light level or sound level over a day and a night.

1 JULY
– gets dark at 9.20pm

1 SEPTEMBER
– gets dark at 7.30pm

1 DECEMBER
– gets dark at 3.55pm

Making it happen

With a sensor connected to a control system, we can make things happen when a certain event or condition happens. So street lights come on when it gets dark enough. They can't be set on a timer, as it gets dark at different times throughout the year.

On and on and on...

In real life, control technology systems keep working 24 hours a day. They are constantly checking the input, so that they can give the right output.

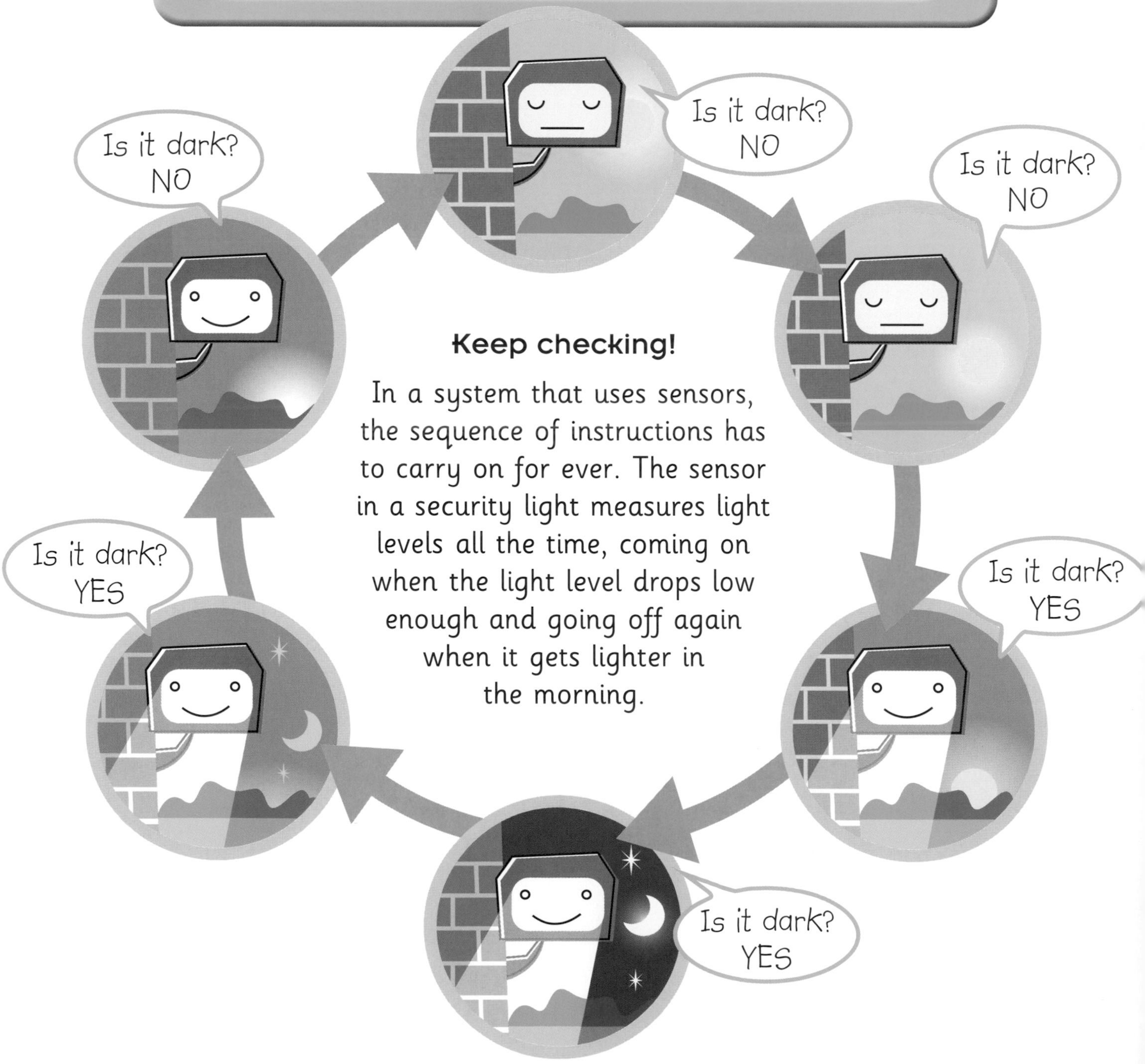

Is it dark?
NO

Is it dark?
NO

Is it dark?
NO

Is it dark?
YES

Is it dark?
YES

Is it dark?
YES

Keep checking!

In a system that uses sensors, the sequence of instructions has to carry on for ever. The sensor in a security light measures light levels all the time, coming on when the light level drops low enough and going off again when it gets lighter in the morning.

When and what?

When designing a system that uses sensors, you need to decide:

- How often you want your system to check the sensors.

- The level of reading that will **trigger** an event.

Regular checks

Some systems don't have to be checked very often. A central heating system could check the temperature in the room every ten or fifteen minutes.

Others need to be more sensitive. A life support system in a hospital, that sounds a buzzer if a patient's heart stops, has to check every few seconds.

What's the trigger?

The system can't decide what you would count as dark or quiet or heavy – you need to pick a level. The central heating could be set to turn on the heating if the temperature falls below, say, 20°C. The life support system could be set to go off if there is no heartbeat for more than three seconds.

Perfect!

You need to test your instructions while you're working on them, and when you've finished, to make sure they do what you set out to do.

Does it work?

As long as you've tested your control sequence step by step as you've built it up, it should all work properly. If not, look for mistakes where you've put the procedures together.

For example, if you end a procedure with 'penup' and don't have a 'pendown' instruction in or before your next procedure, the next one won't draw anything!

Is it what you wanted?

Compare the end result with your original aims. Even if you've followed your plans carefully, you might be able to see a better way. There may be a more direct route for your floor turtle, a simpler procedure to draw the shape you want or a better control sequence.

This way

If your project involves monitoring or sensing, have you chosen the best settings? Is the event triggered at the right time or by the right conditions? Are there any errors in your system?

For example, if you're monitoring temperature, is your sensor sometimes in sunlight and sometimes in shade? If so, move it so that you're always comparing shade temperatures.

Know your limits

It's not always possible to improve the system quite as you'd like. You may be limited by the equipment you have available, or the number of readings you can take.

Even if you can't change these things, it's important that you know what the limits of your system are so that you can work within them.

Projects to try

Now you've learned to understand control sequences and programming, you can try out these fun projects.

Solve a maze

Work with a friend to program a route through a maze.

First find or draw a maze on paper, then work out the instructions to get through it, and write them as a program:

Forward 2
Right 90
Forward 3

...and so on.

If you've got a floor turtle, you could lay out a real maze on the floor and try programming the turtle to move through it.

Finally, one person should read out the instructions for another person to follow. Does it work? If you get stuck, correct the instructions and try again.

If you visit a stately home or garden that has a full-sized maze, try working it out, then sending a friend through it with a set of instructions you've written.

Write your name

If you've got a program like Logo, you can try writing your own name on the screen with it.

It's probably easiest to use capitals, and stick to straight lines. Plan your work first by drawing your name on graph paper or squared paper so that you can count how many steps to take in each direction. Use turns of 45 or 90 degrees.

CARLOS

Even if you don't have a suitable program, you can write the instructions. You could ask a friend to be your screen turtle and follow your instructions with a pen on another piece of squared paper to see if your program works.

Or think big – you could try this project with chalks on a paved playground or brick wall!

Disco lights

Work out a lighting sequence that could be used at a disco. You can use different coloured lights, flashing on or off for a few seconds at a time.

Draw up a storyboard or plan for your sequence, saying which lights are on when and for how long.

Sometimes, a sequence that you think will be fine doesn't work well. If the lights flash too quickly, they can confuse people. If there are intervals of darkness, dancers might crash into each other. Work on improving your sequence.

If you have a control box and some lights, you can then build your sequence and try it out. Does it work? Is it how you expected? Can you improve it?

Not too hot

Try to write a sequence of instructions that you could use to keep your bedroom or your school the right temperature – without wasting money by heating it when no one's there.

You'll need to think about when you're going to be in the room, how long before you get there you want the heating to come on so that it's nice and warm, and what temperature you want it to be.

7.30am – time to get up

9am – gone to school

3.30pm – home from school – time to play

5pm – time for tea and homework

7.30pm – back to bed to read

8.30pm – time to sleep

Take Control and the National Curriculum

This book will help a child to cover work units 4E, 5E, 5F and 6C of the National Curriculum for England and Wales. The National Curriculum for ICT stresses that ICT should be integrated with other areas of study. This means that a child's use of ICT should fit naturally into other areas of the curriculum. It can be achieved by tasks such as:

• Using a sensor connected to the computer to monitor the temperature of a beaker of water in an investigation of the insulation properties of different materials.

• Making variations or rotations of a shape using a screen turtle as part of an art and design project on patterns.

• Comparing the instructions you need for a control sequence with the requirements of instructional text for people to follow.

• Designing a control sequence to operate a security lighting system for the school playground, and building a working model of the system as part of a design and technology project.

Children should incorporate planning, drafting, checking and reviewing their work in all projects. They should discuss with others how their work could be improved, whether ICT methods are the best choice for a given task and how ICT methods compare with manual methods. They should look at ways of combining ICT and manual methods of working.

National Curriculum resources online

ICT programme of study at Key Stage 2 in the National Curriculum:

www.nc.uk.net/

On teaching ICT in other subject areas:

www.ncaction.org.uk/subjects/ict/inother.htm

ICT schemes of work (you can download a printable copy):

www.standards.dfes.gov.uk/schemes2/it/

The schemes of work for Key Stage 2 suggest ways that ICT can be taught in years 3–6.

Further resources

www.blockcorner.com/

An online programming game that lets you build a scene using blocks. Type commands like 'new triangle', 'walk 6', 'paint blue' to define the scene.

http://www.softronix.com/logo.html

Free versions of Logo to download.

Control sequence

Set of instructions that causes something to happen in response to an event.

Control technology

Electronic device or equipment that follows a set of instructions.

Electrical components

Wires, switches, bulbs, buzzers and other pieces of equipment that are used to make electrical circuits.

Input

Information coming in to a computer system.

Logo

Programming language used to control a floor or screen turtle.

Loop

Set of instructions that can be repeated again and again.

Monitoring

Taking regular readings from a sensor to keep track of the state of something, such as the temperature or level of noise.

Output

Information or event that is produced by a computer at the end of a series of instructions.

Procedure

Set of instructions that together make something happen. A procedure is a chunk of a program.

Program (noun)

Set of instructions that make a computer do something.

Programming

Writing instructions to make a computer do something.

Repeat (noun)

Set of instructions that can be repeated again and again.

Sensor

Device for measuring the level of something, such as the temperature or the level of noise, pressure or movement.

Trigger

Make something happen at a particular time.

Index

brackets 13

central heating 23
changes, monitoring 21
checking for mistakes 24-5
checking sensors 22, 23
control sequence 4-5, 31
   input and output 6-7
   testing 24
control technology 4, 20, 22, 31

disco lights project 28
drawing shapes 12-16

electrical components 19, 31
environment 5
   changes in 21
   monitoring 9
equipment 4

floor turtle 8, 10-11, 26

heating 4, 9
house drawings 16

input 6-7, 9, 20, 22, 31
instructions 4, 5, 8-9
   mistakes 16, 17
   naming 13
   repeats 12-13
   for sequences 18-19

testing 16-17, 24-5
   writing 10-13

life support system 23
life support systems 23
light switching 9
Logo 11, 13, 27, 31
loop 12, 16, 31

machines 4
maze project 26
mistakes 16, 17, 24-5
monitoring 9, 21, 25, 31
mystery shape 15

name project 27
number mistakes 17

output 6-7, 9, 22, 31

patterns 14-15
pendown 11, 17, 24
penup 11, 13, 15, 17, 24
procedure 13, 16, 31
programming 8, 31
programs 8
   testing 16-17, 31
projects 26-9

rectangle 14
repeats 12-13, 31

security lights 22
sensors 9, 20-1, 22-3, 31
   checking 22, 23, 25
   connected to computer 21
sequences 18-19
shapes 12-16
snowflakes 15
software 8
spaces 11
spelling mistakes 17
square 12-13
storyboard 19
street lighting 21
supermarket doors 6, 7, 9
switches 20

temperature:
   control 9
   control project 29
   monitoring 21, 25
time sequences 19
traffic lights 18, 19
triangle 14
triggers 20-1, 23, 25, 31
turtle 8, 10-11, 26

windmill 15